EDITH WHARTON

UNIVERSITY OF MINNESOTA

⤳ *Edith Wharton*

BY LOUIS AUCHINCLOSS

UNIVERSITY OF MINNESOTA PRESS · MINNEAPOLIS

Printed in the United States of America at the North Central
Publishing Company, St. Paul

Library of Congress Catalog Card Number: 61-63841

42545
March, 1962

PUBLISHED IN GREAT BRITAIN, INDIA, AND PAKISTAN BY THE OXFORD
UNIVERSITY PRESS, LONDON, BOMBAY, AND KARACHI, AND IN
CANADA BY THOMAS ALLEN, LTD., TORONTO

⹌ Edith Wharton

I⊤ was the fashion among Edith Wharton's friends, initiated by Henry James, to describe her in terms of glowing hyperbole, to see her in the guise of a great golden eagle swooping down from her high built palace of adventure to stir up the poor old croaking barnyard fowls. The woman is almost lost sight of in their boasts of her activities and possessions: the lovingly clipped and tended gardens, the gleaming, perfectly appointed interiors, the big, fast motor (purchased with the proceeds of the current book) bearing its multilingual owner and her faithful band over the roads of Europe to seek out in every nook and cranny the beauty that must redeem a modern wasteland. One imagines rooms refurbished and gardens relandscaped, all over Europe and the American East Coast, to conform with the mandates which she laid down in *The Decoration of Houses* and *Italian Villas and Their Gardens*. Indeed, there are moments when the lady whom Percy Lubbock describes in her Paris garden, fresh and trim, basket on arm, clippers in hand, ready for the daily task of shearing the heads of yesterday's roses, seems but the symbol of a larger self dedicated to sprucing up our very planet.

This is a long way from the picture in the minds of some American critics of a precious and snobbish old lady. Yet one can see how both pictures came into being. Perfection irritates as well as it attracts, in fiction as in life. As some of Mrs. Wharton's acquaintances complained that her taste in furnishing was too good, her French too precisely idiomatic, so have some of her critics found her heroes and heroines too exquisite, too apt to exclaim in rapt unison over little known beauties in art and literature with which

5

the majority of her readers may not be equally familiar. The glittering structure of her cultivation sits on her novels like a rather showy icing that detracts from the cake beneath. That same majority may be put off by descriptions, however vivid, of physical objects and backgrounds that obtrude on the action, by being made to notice, even in scenes of tensest drama, a bit of red damask on a wall, a Jacqueminot rose, a small, dark Italian primitive. As Edmund Wilson points out, Mrs. Wharton was not only the pioneer but the poet of interior decoration.

Such cultivation was certainly not typical of her generation. Ladies of the New York and Newport of her day, educated by tutors, may have acquired a sound basis in German, French, and Italian, but they used these languages, if at all, more for dinner parties than for books. They did not spend their spare time, like Edith Newbold Jones, in their fathers' libraries, nor did they publish, at the age of sixteen, privately printed volumes of poetry. In fact, the very rarity of such intellectual achievement in the family of George Frederic Jones has lent comfort to the bearers of an old legend, totally without foundation, that Edith was the daughter of her brothers' English tutor, a clever young man with a mild painter's talent who was killed in the West by Indians. The theory seems to spring from the same kind of thinking that cannot conceive a Shakespeare born in Stratford. But I find it easier to believe that Lucretia Stevens Rhinelander Jones, granddaughter of a Revolutionary patriot and a conventional society matron in a then small-town New York, should have had a brilliant rather than an illegitimate daughter, and the fact that Edith, being so much younger than her brothers, was brought up like an only child seems adequate explanation for the hours that she spent alone in her father's library in West 23rd Street.

In her memoirs she describes as her good fortune that she was forbidden, on moral grounds, to read the ephemeral rubbish of the day and so was not distracted from the classics on the paternal shelves. It was obvious, she tells us, though I am not sure how quickly we agree, that a little girl "to whom the Old Testament, the Apocalypse and the Elizabethan dramatists were open, could not long pine for Whyte Melville or even Rhoda Broughton." In the sternly impressive list of her early reading, with its heavy emphasis on history and poetry, the only American names are Prescott, Parkman, Longfellow, and Irving. The other Melville, Herman, "a cousin of the Van Rensselaers, and qualified by birth to figure in the best society," she never, as a girl, even heard mentioned. Culture and education, to the Joneses and to their group, still meant Europe.

Europe, however, was not only the fountain of arts; it was also good for one's health and pocketbook. The Joneses were badly hit by the inflation that followed the Civil War and took their little daughter for long, economizing visits to Italy and France. It was a life of hotels and watering places, seeing only fellow Americans and their servants, but there were compensations for a sensitive child in driving out to the Campagna and wandering among the tombs of the Appian Way, in collecting fragments of porphyry and lapis lazuli on the slopes of the Palatine, and in such Parisian sights as the Empress Eugénie in her *daumont*, with the little Prince Imperial at her side and a glittering escort of officers. At the same time the young Henry James was knocking about the continent, staying in pensions and picking up material for his first international tales. On both, the European experience was to have a lasting effect. But what was to have a much greater influence on Edith Jones as a writer, and to supply her with the subject material for her most important work, was neither her father's library nor her early impression of Europe, but her own clear, direct, comprehensive little girl's vision of the New York society in which her parents lived.

In 1862, the year of her birth, and for perhaps two decades thereafter, this was a small, sober, proper, tightly knit society, of Dutch and English descent, which lived in uniform streets of chocolate house fronts on income largely derived from municipal real estate. It was wary of the arts, beyond a dip into Longfellow or Bryant, or an evening of *Norma* at the Academy of Music, and disdainful of politics and any business that smacked of retail. The men practiced law in a listless sort of way and sat on charitable boards and had the leisure and taste to appreciate with their wives long meals of good food washed down by the "Jones Claret" or the "Newbold Madeira." Young Edith, sharply aware of their indifference to beauty in the arts, found their society stifling and stultifying, but as an elderly woman, surrounded by a world that seemed to her to have lost its values, she decided ruefully that the merit of those "amiable persons" had been to uphold standards of education and good manners and of scrupulous probity in business and private affairs.

As a young girl and as a debutante, she was miserably shy, a quality that was to dog her all her life, and that she was later to encase behind the enamel of formality, but by the time of her marriage, at the age of twenty-three, she had become at least outwardly reconciled to the observances of social life. Edward Robbins Wharton was an easygoing, friendly Bostonian, of no intellectual pretensions, who adored his much younger wife and always kept a thousand dollar bill in his purse in case "Pussy" wanted anything. They lived in New York and Newport and went every year to Europe, and no children came to interrupt their social and sightseeing routine. Obviously, it was not an existence to satisfy indefinitely a mind rendered immune to Rhoda Broughton by the beauties of the Apocalypse, and gradually the young wife started to write, here and there a poem, then a sentimental short story with an uplifting conclusion, then a serious book on interior decoration, then travel pieces, at last a historical novel. In her memoirs she describes her writing as the natural sequence of a childhood habit of "making up" on bits of brown wrapping paper, but Edmund Wilson suggests that she took it up because of the tensions of an incompatible marriage and at the advice of Dr. S. Weir Mitchell, an early pioneer in female neuroses and himself a novelist. Fragments of her diary, recently published by Wayne Andrews, in which she notes that she could endure the "moral solitude" of her marriage only by creating a world of her imagination, certainly seem to substantiate Wilson. At any rate, there was the gap of a generation between those brown paper scribblings and the publication of her first volume of fiction at the age of thirty-seven.

The tales in *The Greater Inclination* (1899) and in its successor, *Crucial Instances* (1901), have some of the flavor of James's stories of artists and writers of the same period. They are apt to be set against European backgrounds and to deal with such themes as the temptation to the serious artist of commercial success or the bewildering influence upon him of the art of an older, richer civilization. They are clever and readable, if a trifle thin, and in three of them, "The Pelican," "The Rembrandt," and "The Angel at the Grave," Mrs. Wharton shows herself already in full command of the style that was to make her prose as lucid and polished as any in American fiction. It is a firm, crisp, smooth, direct, easily flowing style, the perfect instrument of a clear, undazzled eye, an analytic mind, and a sense of humor alert to the least pretentiousness. We may later wonder if her style was adapted to all the uses to which she put it, but at this point it perfectly presents to us, in all their pathetic and confused dignity, the brave little lady who lectures with an ignorant boldness to women's groups on every aspect of arts and letters, first for the love of her baby and ultimately for the love of her own voice, the proud and splendid widow who is induced only by direst poverty to part with her false Rem-

9

brandt, and the dedicated spinster who devotes a lifetime to maintaining her grandfather's house as a shrine for a public that has forgotten him. The defect in Edith Wharton's poetry, of which she published three volumes, is that this same style, consciously ennobled and stripped of laughter, becomes as dull and overornamented as the privately printed verse of any number of aspiring ladies who sought refuge from the distraction of social life. But poetry is subjective, and Mrs. Wharton, like many persons of wide reading and disciplined exterior, was inclined to be mawkish in subjective mood.

Her first novel, *The Valley of Decision*, appeared in 1902, when she was forty, and its scene is laid in Italy, that charnel house of English and American historical fiction. It is Edith Wharton's *Romola*, except that it is a better book than George Eliot's, for the fruits of her research are strewn attractively through the pages and not spooned into the reader like medicine. But although she captures remarkably the spirit and color of the eighteenth century, nothing can save the novel from its pale and lifeless characters. It is like a play with perfect settings in which the actors stand stiffly in the middle of the stage, their eyes fixed on the prompter. Only when Odo as a boy visits his grandfather's castle in the mountains, and later in the grand ducal gallery when he faces the portraits of his interbred ancestors, is there any true linking of characters and sets. The theme, however, is of some interest to the student of Edith Wharton, for it presages the political and social conservatism that was later to enchain her. Odo brings reform to Pianura only to find himself the harbinger and later the prisoner of the Reign of Terror. His creator was always afraid that even a needed cleaning of sewers might cause the collapse of the civilization above them.

The next two years find Mrs. Wharton still experimenting. *Sanctuary* (1903) demonstrates, a bit comically, the combined influence of Paul Bourget and James. In the first part of this absurd but charming little tale Kate Peyton marries a cheat and a liar in order to become the mother of the moral defective whom he might otherwise sire upon a woman less capable of raising such offspring — surely almost a parody of a Bourget theme — and in the second, twenty-five years later, she contrives to keep this offspring from committing an odious fraud by radiating sympathy to him in silent Jamesian waves. *The Descent of Man* (1904) is another volume of short stories, similar in tone to the earlier ones except for "The Dilettante," which marks an advance in the development of a male character who is to pervade all of Mrs. Wharton's fiction, the cold, cultivated, aristocratic egoist who feeds on the life and enthusiasm of simpler souls. The story has a clever twist at the end when the dilettante's betrothed jilts him on discovering that the lady who has been his intimate friend for years has *not* been his mistress. It is a theme that we shall meet again.

The House of Mirth (1905) marks her coming of age as a novelist. At last, and simultaneously, she had discovered both her medium and her subject matter. The first was the novel of manners and the latter the assault upon the old Knickerbocker society in which she had grown up of the new millionaires, the "invaders" as she called them, who had been so fabulously enriched by the business growth following the Civil War. New money had poured into New York in the 1880's and 1890's and turned the Joneses' quiet old Fifth Avenue into a dizzy parade of derivative façades from Azay-le-Rideau to the Porch of the Maidens. The Van Rensselaers and Rhinelanders might purse their lips at the ostentation of the Vanderbilts, but in a dollar world the biggest bank balance was bound to win out. A Livingston would marry a Mills, as in an earlier day a Schermerhorn had married an Astor. For what, really, did that older world have that was so special? It was all very well for James to describe the Newport of his childhood, surviving into this gilded age, as a little bare white open hand suddenly crammed with gold, but the fingers of that little hand closed firmly enough over the proffered bullion. The sober brown stucco of Upjohn's country villas concealed a materialism as rampant as any flaunted by the marble halls of Richard Morris Hunt. Mrs. Wharton saw clearly enough that the invaders and defenders were bound ultimately to bury their hatchet in a noisy, stamping dance, but she saw also the rich possibilities for satire in the contrasts afforded by the battle line in its last stages and the pathos of the individuals who were fated to be trampled under the feet of those boisterous truce makers.

Lily Bart, the heroine of *The House of Mirth*, stems from both worlds. Her father is related to the Penistons and the Stepneys, but is driven by her mother, a more ordinary creature, to make a fortune which, not being of invader blood, he is bound to lose. Lily, orphaned, is loosed on the social seas with only her beauty and charm for sails and no rudder but a ladylike disdain for shabby compromises and a vague sense that there must be somewhere a better life than the one into which she has drifted. Her rich friends, who use her as a social secretary to write notes and as a blind to shield them from importunate and suspicious husbands, cannot understand the squeamishness which keeps her, at the critical moment, from extracting a proposal from the rich bachelor whom she has not been too squeamish to pursue. Her respectable relatives, on the other hand, of an older society, cannot understand her smoking or gambling or being seen, however briefly, in the company of married men. Lily falls between two stools. She cannot bring herself to marry the vulgar Mr. Rosedale for all his millions, or the obscure Lawrence Selden, for all their affinity. She postpones decisions and hopes for the best and in the meanwhile seeks to distract herself. But we know from the start that she is doomed. She has only her loveliness, and what is that in a world that puts its store in coin and hypocrisy? The other characters, of both new and old New York, seem strangely and vindictively united in a constant readiness to humiliate her: Grace Stepney to tell tales on her, Mrs. Peniston to disinherit her, Bertha Dorset to abandon her in a foreign port, Gus Trenor to try to seduce her, his wife to say he has. We watch with agonized apprehension as Lily turns and doubles back, as she keeps miraculously rehabilitating herself, each time on a slightly lower level. For no matter how hard she struggles, without money she is unarmed in that arena. And in the end when she finally compromises and is willing to marry Rosedale, it is too late. He will not have her, and she falls to the job at the milliner's and the ultimate overdose of sleeping tablets. But we finish the book with the conviction that in the whole brawling, terrible city Lily is the one and only lady.

The different levels of society in *The House of Mirth* are explored with a precision comparable to that of Proust whom Mrs. Wharton was later so greatly to admire. We follow Lily's gradual descent from "Bellomont" on the Hudson and the other great country houses of a world where the old and new societies had begun to merge, to the little court of the Gormers, who, although rich enough to be ultimately accepted, are still at the stage of having to fill their house with hangers-on, to the bogus intellectual world of Carry Fisher who pretends to like interesting people while she earns her living helping climbers up the social ladder, to the final drop into the gilded hotel of the demimondaine Norma Hatch. Lily learns that money is the common denominator of all these worlds and that the differences between them consist only in the degrees of scent with which its odor is from time to time concealed. Van Wyck Brooks accused Mrs. Wharton of knowing nothing of the American West, and perhaps she did not, but she had a firsthand knowledge of where the profits of the frontier had gone. Lily Bart, weary on foot, watching the carriages and motors of her former friends ply up and down Fifth Avenue, Mrs. Van Osburgh's C-spring barouche, Mrs. Hatch's electric victoria, is seeing the natural successors of the covered wagon.

I do not suppose that Mrs. Wharton intended Lawrence Selden to constitute the last and greatest of Lily's trials, but so he strikes me. He is a well-born, leisurely bachelor lawyer, with means just adequate for a life of elegant solitude, who spends his evenings, when not leafing through the pages of his first editions, dining out in a society that he loves to ridicule. Lily knows that he is a neutral in the battle of life and death in which she is so desperately engaged, and she asks only that he hold her hand briefly in moments of crisis or brush her lips with a light kiss. He does, in the end, decide to marry her, but as she has been too late for Rosedale, so is he too late for her, and he can only kneel by her bed and give to her lifeless lips the last of his airy kisses. Mrs. Wharton's attitude toward Selden's type of man is enigmatic. He may be a villain in "The Dilettante," or he may at least pose as a hero in *The House of Mirth*. She is careful in the latter to point out for his sake, whenever he condemns Lily Bart, that appearances have been against her. Perhaps she conceived him as an abused lover in the Shakespearean sense, as an Othello or a Posthumus. But Othello and Posthumus are quick to believe the worst because of the very violence of their passions. An eye as dry as Selden's should be slower to be deceived. I incline to the theory that Mrs. Wharton really intended us to accept this plaster-cast figure for a hero, but that she had a low opinion of heroes in general. When Lily suddenly retorts to Selden that he spends a great deal of his time in a society that he professes to despise, it is as if the author had suddenly slipped into the book to express a contempt that the reader is not meant to share.

The enigma of Selden inevitably leads to a consideration of the deepest friendship of Edith Wharton's life. "The year before my marriage," she relates in her memoirs, "I had made friends with a young man named Walter Berry, the son of an old friend of my family's (and indeed a distant cousin)." Despite the note of kinship thus cautiously sounded, there is a legend that he proposed to her and was turned down as a not good enough match. This might, if true, explain in the light of revenge some of his acts of coldness to her in later years. At any rate, he became a friend of the young Whartons, and it was during one of his visits to their house in Newport that she showed him the "lumpy pages" of an early manuscript and had the mortification of hearing his "shout of laughter," a peal that was never quite to cease ringing in her ears. But a minute later he said good-naturedly: "Come, let's see what can be done," and settled down beside her to try to model the lump into a book. In that modeling process she claimed, decades later, that she had been taught whatever she knew about the writing of "clear concise English."

I do not believe it, though I am sure that she did. There seemed no limits to her admiration of Berry. "He found me when my mind and soul were hungry and thirsty, and he fed them till our last hour together." Evidently, he supplied her with the intellectual and spiritual companionship that she had never found with Edward Wharton. The latter, as her writing and fame developed, had shrunk to a kind of cipher in her life. Consuelo Balsan recalls him "as more of an equerry than an equal, walking behind her and carrying whatever paraphernalia she happened to discard." It was only to be expected, under the circumstances, that she should fall in love with Berry, yet it is not until 1908, when she was forty-six, that her journal begins to evidence it. "I should like to be to you, friend of my heart, like a touch of wings brushing by you in the darkness, or like the scent of an invisible garden that one passes by on an unknown road." The tone of this and other entries would seem to confirm the opinion of many of those close to her that she received only friendship in return. Berry, according to them, was perfectly willing to let her play her chosen role of the touch of wings or the invisible garden. But these, of course, had been only phrases. Like any woman, she wanted more: "You hurt me — you disillusioned me — and when you left me, I was more deeply yours." When he went to Cairo to be a judge of the International Tribunal, she could hardly endure it: "Oh, my adored, my own love, you who have given me the only moments of real life I have ever known, how am I to face the long hours and days?" But she did face them, and one wonders if correspondence with so tepid an admirer might not have been simpler in the end than talks and scenes.

What sort of man was he? James seems to have liked him and to have enjoyed their faintly catty old bachelors' correspondence in which Mrs. Wharton, because of her raids into the secluded retreats of friends, is described as "the angel of devastation." But to others of her circle Berry was less sympathetic, and to Percy Lubbock he was a dogmatic and snobbish egotist, the evil genius, indeed, of her life. "None of her friends," he put it bluntly, "thought she was the better for the surrender of her fine free spirit to the control of a man, I am ready to believe, of strong intelligence and ability — but also, I certainly know, of a dry and narrow and supercilious temper."

Mrs. Wharton's attitude toward evasion of the marriage vow was always ambiguous. Divorce (though she was to come to it herself) she considered crude and antisocial, and the facile forming of new marital ties unspeakably vulgar. On the other hand, the dishonesties and evasions of concealed adultery struck her as offensive and degrading, while any open disregard of the conventions led to a slow, sordid end in those shabby European watering places with which the minds of her contemporaries seemed always to identify extramarital passion. Perhaps, finally, the latter course seemed best to her. At least the spirit that was capable of facing it seemed the finest spirit. Paulina Trant in "The Long Run" (*Xingu*) has all her creator's sympathy when she offers to give up her husband and home for love, and Halston Merrick, who logically and sensibly tries to reason her out of it, appears as the shallowest of lovers. There must have been womanly moments, for all of Edith Wharton's admiration of Berry, when he struck her as a bit of a Halston Merrick, when she saw him with eyes that made even Lubbock's seem charitable by comparison. It is perhaps to such moments that we owe the curious ambivalence in her treatment of heroes.

Despite the great critical and popular success of *The House of Mirth*, Mrs. Wharton did not return to her New York subject matter for another eight years. Perhaps she was afraid of exhausting it too quickly. *Madame de Treymes* and *The Fruit of the Tree*, so radically different from each other, both appeared in 1907. The first is a true Jamesian tale of innocents abroad, as subtle and fine as any of James's own but with more liveliness and humor. It portrays the duel between John Durham, an American hero in the tradition of James's Christopher Newman, and a wily, charming Parisian aristocrat, Madame de Treymes, over the latter's sister-in-law, poor little Fanny Frisbee of brownstone New York, who has found only misery in her French marriage. Principles and ideals, for the last time in Edith Wharton's fiction, are found on the side of the Stars and Stripes, and Madame de Treymes ruefully recognizes the moral superiority of the Yankee in her final sob: "Ah, you poor, good man!" In later years, unhappily, Mrs. Wharton's Americans abroad were to become the corrupters and not the corrupted.

The Fruit of the Tree is an experiment in a totally new field, the novel of reform. Mrs. Wharton began her task of research conscientiously enough with a tour of a factory near her country home in Lenox, Massachusetts, but she soon lost interest in her theme and succumbed to an unworthy compromise. In order to be able to draw her factory manager and trained nurse from models in her own world, she endowed them both with old and distinguished families which had only recently lost their money, thus giving to these parts of her book a curious air of social masquerade. Even so, the reader's interest is caught when Amherst, the priggish manager, marries the widow owner of the factory, having misconstrued her passion for himself as a zeal for the cause of the workers, and settles down in blithe ignorance to what he imagines will be their shared task of reform. But at this point Mrs. Wharton changes her theme altogether. Bessie Amherst, bored with the workers and interpreting, perhaps correctly (again the enigma of the Wharton hero), her husband's interest in reform as indifference to herself, goes galloping over icy roads until she falls from her horse and receives an incurable back injury, which condemns her to a long period of hideous and futile agony. The novel now turns abruptly into a problem novel about euthanasia in the manner of Bourget, for Bessie's sufferings are abbreviated by the needle of the trained nurse with the social background. Mrs. Wharton handles both themes competently, but the book simply collapses between them. The failure of *The Fruit of the Tree* is just the opposite of that of *The Valley of Decision*; the settings, and not the characters, fade away. It is, however, a less disastrous fault. Bessie Amherst, indolent, selfish, but quite ready to be led by any man who will take the trouble to understand her, is interesting enough to make the novel readable even today, when industrial reform of the type in question has long since been effected and when euthanasia, if still illegal, has ceased to be morally shocking.

The Hermit and the Wild Woman (1908) is another volume of slender, contrived Jamesian stories of artists and dilettantes, but *Tales of Men and Ghosts* (1910) contains some superb chillers. A tricky ending to a serious short story will sometimes detract from the total effect and make it seem superficial or sentimental, or both, but in a ghost story it has a valid, even an indispensable, function. The egotism of Mrs. Wharton's constantly recurring bachelors is brought out more effectively in "The Eyes" than in any of her other short stories or novels. Culwin tells a listening group about a fire, which includes his young protégé, of the eyes, the old eyes with sunk orbits and thick, red-lined lids and look of vicious security, that haunt him at night whenever he has performed what he deems an unselfish act, which the reader, of course, knows to have been just the opposite. As he finishes his tale he marks the horror on the features of the protégé, with whose youth and bloom he has tried to water his own dry nature, and turning to look in the mirror behind him, he sees at last whose eyes they are.

Mrs. Wharton's other ghost stories may be considered out of chronology because their style and effectiveness does not vary, except to improve, with the years. This kind of tale requires a skill that never left her, the skill of telling a story reduced to its bare bones, without the aid of social problems or manners or mores or even of human nature, except in its most elemental sense. She always believed that the storytelling faculty was basic and indispensable in any writer. She was like a representational artist who looks askance at an abstract painting and wants to know if the man who executed it can really draw. At times she would try her hand, almost as one might try a puzzle, at a story that was nothing but technique, like "Roman Fever," where the interest and excitement is concentrated in the last line that gives the whole meaning to what has gone before. Her technique in ghost stories is to keep the supernatural to the minimum that will still irradiate the tale with horror. Character can be important as in "The Eyes," but it is by no means essential. As long as there is one plain human being, as in "All Souls," to register terror for the reader, there is an adequate cast.

Time, as we shall see, brought to Mrs. Wharton an attitude of disapproval toward the changing social scene which was to sour her later work, but the ghost stories, by their very nature, escaped this, and her grasp of the secret of chilling her reader continued to improve to the end. "The Lady's Maid's Bell," an early venture, suffers from a slight overdose of the eerie. There is not only the bell; there is the constantly reappearing ghost of Emma Saxon. "Pomegranate Seed," a later tale, corrects this. A second wife's happiness is destroyed and her life turned to nightmare by the appearance, at irregular intervals, on the hall table, addressed to her husband in a faint, female handwriting, of envelopes which unnerve him but which he refuses to discuss. The conviction that these missives come from the dead wife begins to dawn on the reader at the same time that it dawns on her successor, and in the mood of horror that we share with her we completely accept her husband's final disappearance. The ghost of the first wife never comes on the scene to derogate from her letters as Emma Saxon does from the bell.

In the compilation *Ghosts* (1937), published in the last year of Mrs. Wharton's life, two of the best of the eleven stories, "Miss Mary Pask" and "Bewitched," deal, not with the supernatural, but with the appearance of it. Here Mrs. Wharton sets herself the difficult task of scaring the reader in a ghost story without the aid of a ghost. The atmosphere has to be made correspondingly more ominous; Mary Pask must be whiter and more wraithlike on that foggy night in Brittany than if she were a true spirit, and the New Englanders of "Bewitched" must be gaunter and grimmer than the characters of *Ethan Frome* to make sufficiently terrible the ending that proves Venny Brand to have been masquerading. The last story of the collection, and its masterpiece, "A Bottle of Perrier," is not really a ghost story at all, but a tale of hatred and murder in the African desert where an eccentric Englishman lives in a lonely castle with his butler and a host of Arab servants. Mrs. Wharton's style is at its richest as she sets her African scene: "The afternoon hung over the place like a great velarium of cloth-of-gold stretched across the battlements and drooping down in ever slacker folds upon the heavy-headed palms. When at length the gold turned to violet, and the west to a bow of crystal clasping the dark sands, Medford shook off his sleep and wandered out." And the final sentence which reveals for the reader where the body of Almodham has all the time been rotting is like one of those screaming chords at the end of Strauss's *Salome*: "The moon, swinging high above the battlements, sent a searching spear of light down into the guilty darkness of the well."

In 1911 Mrs. Wharton published the short novel with which her name has ever since been linked and which sometimes threatens to preempt the whole of her niche in the history of American literature. She says in her memoirs that in writing *Ethan Frome*, she felt for the first time the artisan's full control of his implements. In later years its continuing success was to plague her, as the success of "Daisy Miller" plagued James, for she could never agree with the critics who claimed that it was her best work. Yet it is surely among her best. When I think of it, I visualize a small painting, perfectly executed to the last detail, of three silent figures in a small dark cottage kitchen, with snow glimpsed through a window, the terrible Zeena in the center, white and pasty and gaunt, and, scattered on the table, the pieces of a broken dish. But I could never put the story as fiction in the same class with *The House of Mirth* on the very ground that to me it *is* a picture and, as such, one dimensional. Lily Bart and the society in which she lives are turned around and around and studied from different angles. It is not fair, of course, to compare a long novel with a novelette, but the tremendous reputation of *Ethan Frome* evokes such a defense.

There has been some disposition in critics to view with distrust

Mrs. Wharton's excursions into life among the needy, as evidenced by *Ethan Frome,* "The Bunner Sisters," and *Summer,* to see her as the great lady from "The Mount" in Lenox, peering at Ethan and his womenfolk from the back seat of her big motor. I doubt if these comments would have been made had the stories been published under another name, for the keenness of Mrs. Wharton's observation was not affected by the social status of her models. Only, in later years, when she attempted to describe persons and places that she had never seen did she fail in her job. I am totally persuaded of the reality of that notions shop kept by Ann Eliza Bunner and her sister and by the dank public library where Charity Royall dreams away her listless days. The reason why *Summer* and "The Bunner Sisters" are less convincing than *Ethan Frome* does not lie in any failure of observation or imagination on the part of the author, but in the fact that one feels her presence, which in *Ethan Frome* the device of a narrator has successfully eliminated. When Charity Royall sees her mother's kinfolk on the mountain "herded together in a sort of passive promiscuity in which their common misery was the strongest link," and when Evalina Bunner, contrasted to the Hochmullers, is described as "a faintly washed sketch beside a brilliant chromo," we see clearly enough what is meant, but we are standing on that mountain and at Evalina's wedding with Mrs. Wharton herself, and we feel with a touch of constraint the incongruity of our presence.

The Reef (1912) was greeted with a burst of congratulation from all the Jamesian circle. "Racinian" was the adjective used by the master, and indeed a Racinian unity of mood is achieved by centering the action in an old, high-roofed chateau of brick and yellowish stone, bathed in the pale light of October afternoons. The rooms in which the characters tensely talk are like a series of paintings by Walter Gay. It is a quiet, controlled, beautiful novel, but its theme has always struck me as faintly ridiculous. Mrs. Leath, a widow, is at last about to marry George Darrow, her old bachelor admirer, and her stepson, Owen, is entertaining a similar plan with respect to the beautiful young family governess, Sophy Viner, when the discovery that Darrow and Sophy have once been lovers reduces all the characters to a state of quiet desperation. Even conceding that in 1912 such an affair might have disqualified Sophy as a bride for Owen, would Mrs. Leath, a woman who had lived all her adult years in France, consider that her own happiness had to be sacrificed as well? Of course, Mrs. Wharton's answer would be that Mrs. Leath is a woman of the finest sensitivities and that the affair occurred at a time when she had every reason to believe Darrow attentive to herself, but I still cannot get away from the suspicion that at least part of the horror of the situation lies in the fact that Sophy is a governess. The final chapter, so jarringly out of tune with the rest of the book, tends to confirm this suspicion. When Mrs. Leath goes to Sophy's sister's hotel to tell Sophy that she has given Darrow up, she is received by the sister in a dim, untidy, scented room, complete with lover and masseur. Coarse and bloated as the sister is, Mrs. Leath can nonetheless see in her what the beautiful Sophy will one day become, and when she discovers that the latter has departed for India in the company of a disreputable woman, she takes her hasty leave, presumably to return to Darrow and happiness.

The only moral that I can make out of this is that Sophy Viner, a paid dependent who is an appendage rather than a true part of the social pattern, may be expected, under the first bad influence, to drop to a life of semi-prostitution. If the problem to which the book is addressed be justified as a problem common to the era, there remains to be justified the point of view of the author, which for once seems as narrowly prudish and class-conscious as her bitterest critics have ever accused it of being.

The Custom of the Country, happily, in the following year, 1913, is a return to the rich, sure ground of New York and the novel of manners, only this time the central character in the conflict of social groups is not a victim but an invader. Undine Spragg is a creature of alloy, as sentimental in her judgments of herself as she is ruthless in her judgments of others. A father is only a checkbook, a husband a means of social advancement, a baby a threat to the figure. No amount of association with cultivated persons or of exposure to the art of Europe can ripple the surface of her infinite vulgarity. She never knows the toll in human misery of her advance to the social heights, for it never occurs to her to look back. The story of how she hews her way through the old New York ranks of the Marvells and Dagonets, already weakened by prior compromises with the invaders, and even into the society of the Faubourg Saint-Germain from which James's "American" was barred, is vivid and fascinating. Undine gets into as many dangerous corners as Lily Bart, but by miscalculation rather than by inertia, and the same shrewd, restless cerebration that gets her in can be counted on to get her out. In *The House of Mirth* our compassion goes out to Lily; in *The Custom of the Country* it goes out to the society which Undine is trying to crash.

The flaw in the novel that keeps it from ranking equally with its predecessor is that Mrs. Wharton hates Undine too much. She sees in her incarnate the devil of the modern world, that world where all fineness of soul and graciousness of living has been submerged in a great tide of insipid and meretricious uniformity whose origin seems to lie vaguely in the American Middle West. New York has been lost to the flood, and even Europe is no longer safe. The family of the Marquis de Chelles are not sufficiently humiliated by his marriage to Undine; they must also see their tapestries stripped from their walls by her next husband, Elmer Moffatt. What would the wiles of even Madame de Treymes have accomplished against Elmer? James complained to Mrs. Wharton that she had not sufficiently developed the theme of the relation-ship between the Chelleses and Undine. Surely, he was wrong. Surely, as the book indicates, no such relationship could have even existed. What Mrs. Wharton fails to prove is that Chelles would have married Undine at all. For she is really too awful to be quite so successful with quite so many men. Her vulgarity destroys the allure that such a woman would have been bound to have and that her creator was not to understand until her last, unfinished novel.

Lily Bart takes only one trip to Europe in the course of her saga, but Undine spends half of hers there. It was abroad, indeed, that Mrs. Wharton must have observed her prototypes, for in these years she had been spending less and less time in her own country. She had always been attracted by the order and grace of French living and by the assured social position of intellectuals in France, so different from what she had experienced in New York. She had a deep respect for traditions and ceremonials that gave her some assurance that the existing form of society had a basis in the past, and, by a like token, a hope for preservation in the future. The New York of her younger years had had traditions, but she had found them merely restricting. The dead hand of a Manhattan past had seemed to her simply dead. Her writing, for example, had never been recognized by her friends and relations as anything but a vaguely embarrassing habit that was better not mentioned. Her husband, it was true, took a rather childish pride in her grow-ing fame, but in all intellectual matters he was as bad as the others. "Does that sort of thing really amuse you?" he asked when she showed him a striking passage in R. H. Lock's study of heredity and variation. "That is the answer to everything worth-while!" she moaned in her journal. "Oh, Gods of derision! And you've given me twenty years of it! *Je n'en peux plus.*"

This cry of the heart is dated 1908 when she was forty-six. Re-lease was on its way. In 1910 the Whartons sold the house in Lenox and moved permanently to France. In the same year Edward Wharton had a nervous collapse and was placed in a sanatorium. In 1913 they were divorced. She had found at last a world where everything blended: beautiful surroundings, intellectual companionship, a society that combined a respect for the past with a vital concern for the present. London was within easy reach, and she could be in constant touch with writers whose conversation was as polished and civilized as their prose: James, Bourget, Lubbock, Howard Sturgis. It is easy to comprehend the charm of such a life, but what did it have to do with the contemporary American scene that it was her profession to study? James in his later years built his characters into an exotic world of his own imagination. It was not necessary for the creator of Maggie Verver or Millie Theale to have an up-to-date knowledge of life on the other side of the Atlantic. It was enough that he had been born American. But Edith Wharton was concerned with representing the life and manners of New York, and for this she needed more than the chatter of tourist friends.

In a surprisingly insipid little book, *French Ways and Their Meaning* (1919), made up of articles originally written to acquaint Americans coming to France during the war with the character of their allies and hosts, Mrs. Wharton descants on the Gallic qualities of taste, reverence, continuity, and intellectual honesty. The picture that emerges, quite unintentionally, is of a nation chained to ancient forms and observances which could hardly have survived four years of trench warfare with the first military power of Europe. Mrs. Wharton was paying France what she deemed the greatest compliment she knew in describing as national virtues the qualities that most attracted her in her own polite, intellectual circle. There is some of the self-justification of the expatriate in the attitude that her adopted country had to possess to the fullest degree, and her native land to the least, the civilized atmosphere which she found so indispensable in daily life. As a result, there was always a presumption in favor of France in her thinking, just as there was one against America, an injustice that is everywhere reflected in this misleading little book. When she speaks of French culture, Richelieu and the Academy are invoked, but when it is a question of American, she cites only the middle western college girl who "learnt art" in a year.

When crisis came, at any rate, she had proved a true, if not a legal, citizen of France. She scorned the expatriates who scuttled home at the first rumble of danger in the summer of 1914 and whom she later described in *The Marne*. She was passionately involved from the beginning with the land of her adoption and threw herself into work for the refugees and the wounded with a fervor and efficiency which resulted in her being decorated by Poincaré and named an officer of the Legion of Honor. She regarded the war from a simple but consistent point of view: France, virtually singlehanded, was fighting the battle of civilization against the powers of darkness. It was the spirit that made men fight and die, but it has never, unfortunately, been the spirit of fiction. Reading *The Marne* (1918) and *A Son at the Front* (1923) today gives one the feeling of taking an old enlistment poster out of an attic trunk. It may be a significant comment on the very nature of Armageddon that the only literature that survives it is literature of disillusionment and despair. Mrs. Wharton knew that the war was terrible; she had visited hospitals and even the front itself. But the exhilaration of the noncombatant, no matter how dedicated and useful her services, has a shrill sound to postwar ears.

The corrosive effect of war on a civilization already vulgarized by American money induced in Mrs. Wharton a mood of nostalgia for the old quiet New York world of her childhood that she had once found so confining. Much later she was to write: "When I was young it used to seem to me that the group in which I grew up was like an empty vessel into which no new wine would ever again be poured. Now I see that one of its uses lay in preserving a few drops of an old vintage too rare to be savoured by a youthful palate."

There was no rose color, however, in the glasses through which she viewed the past. She did not flinch at sight of the old prejudices; she simply reinterpreted them. Mrs. Lidcote, in "Autre Temps" (*Xingu*, 1916) has been ostracized for leaving her husband for a lover, but when she returns to New York, a generation later, to take her stand by her daughter who has done the same thing, she discovers that times have changed and that her daughter can now marry her lover and be received by the very people who have cut Mrs. Lidcote. The times, however, have changed only for the daughter's generation. Society will not revise its judgments of individuals, and Mrs. Lidcote must dine upstairs on a tray in order not to embarrass a dinner party gathered to beam on the young lovers. But there is another, subtler moral in the story, and that is in the suggestion that Mrs. Lidcote, with all her suffering, has had a richer life than her daughter with her easy divorce and remarriage. She may feel like a lonely anachronism as she returns to her exile in Europe, but there is no envy in her reflections: "Where indeed in this crowded, topsy-turvy world, with its headlong changes and helter-skelter readjustments, its new tolerances and indifferences and accommodations, was there room for a character fashioned by slower sterner processes and a life broken under their inexorable pressure?"

But this is nostalgia for the very brand that did the burning! Ten years later, in *Twilight Sleep*, Mrs. Wharton was to go even further in her stand against the vapid painlessness of the postwar world by ridiculing the heavy doping of mothers in childbirth. The past came to have a certain validity to her simply by being the

past. The New York of her childhood, that "cramped horizonta
gridiron of a town without towers, porticoes, fountains or perspec
tives, hide-bound in its deadly uniformity of mean ugliness," hav
ing vanished, became as fascinating as Atlantis or Troy. It is to th
attitude of apology toward her parents' generation that we owe he
finest novel.

The title, *The Age of Innocence,* refers to the New York of the
1870's in the girlhood of Edith Jones and gives to the book the
flavor of a historical novel, as is often pointed out by critics. The
fact not always recognized by critics is that it was a habit of Vic-
torian novelists to set their stories in the era of their childhood.
The novelist of manners has since shown a tendency to revert to
a usually recent past where social distinctions, which make up so
much of his subject matter, were more sharply defined, or at least
where he thinks they were. *The Age of Innocence* (1920) is written
in a Proustian mood of remembered things that evokes the airless
atmosphere of an old, ordered, small-town New York as vividly as
a conversation piece by Eastman Johnson. Here the dilettante
bachelor, Newland Archer, as usual a lawyer, is at last placed in
a story adapted to bring out the best and the worst in him. For
he must have enough passion and imagination to aspire to break
through the barriers of convention that surround him and yet be
weak enough so that he cannot finally escape the steely embrace of
an aroused tribe. Newland knows that he never really has a chance
from the beginning; that is his pathos. He is engaged to May Welland, and he will marry May Welland and spend a lifetime with
May Welland, and that is that, and both he and May's beautiful,
Europeanized, disenchanted cousin, Ellen Olenska, realize it and
accept it.

We have a suffocating sense of a creature trapped and doomed
as poor Newland comes to the awareness, from the exchanged
glances, coughs, and silences that surround him, that all of his

vast family and family-in-law, including his own wife, are convinced that he is enjoying the very affair that he has failed to achieve and are united in irresistible tact to cut it short. But Mrs. Wharton is not suggesting that Newland and Ellen, in their renunciation of each other, have condemned themselves to a life of unrewarding frustration. Rules and regulations have now their validity to her, no matter what passions they crush. "It was you," Ellen tells Archer, "who made me understand that under the dullness there are things so fine and sensitive and delicate that even those I most cared for in my other life look cheap in comparison." And a generation later Archer sees no cause to repine in thinking back over his married life with May: "Their long years together had shown him that it did not so much matter if marriage was a dull duty, as long as it kept the dignity of a duty: lapsing from that, it became a mere battle of ugly appetites. Looking about him, he honored his own past, and mourned for it. After all, there was good in the old ways."

It is Edith Wharton's tribute to her own background, this affirmation that under the thick, smoky glass of convention bloom the fine, fragile flowers of patient suffering and self-sacrifice. To run away from society may be as vulgar in the end as to crash it. Newland Archer builds a shrine in his heart around the image of Ellen from which he derives strength to endure his uneventful and moderately useful life, a life where civic and social duties are judiciously balanced and where the impetus of Theodore Roosevelt even gets him into the state legislature, if only for a single term. We see him more completely than any other of Mrs. Wharton's heroes, and the reader who doubts that such a type existed has only to turn the pages of the voluminous diary of George Templeton Strong, published long after Edith Wharton's death.

The comparison with Strong's diary is also relevant in that *The Age of Innocence* is the first of Mrs. Wharton's novels to have all the action seen through the eyes of one character. The interest is thus centered in Newland Archer, as the interest in the two later books where she used the same method, *The Mother's Recompense* and *The Children*, is centered in Kate Clephane and Martin Boyne. Unlike James, however, she refused to be limited in her own comments to her central character's point of view. Archer's conventional way of looking at life, at least in the first half of the book, is too dull a lens for the reader, and his creator never hesitates to peer over his shoulder and point out all kinds of interesting things on the New York scene that we would otherwise miss. James would have objected to this. He would have argued that the spiritual growth of Archer, like that of Lambert Strether in *The Ambassadors*, would have a richer significance if viewed entirely through Archer's mind. It was one of their principal points of division. Mrs. Wharton refused to subordinate to any rule of design the "irregular and irrelevant movements of life" that to her made up the background of her stories.

It is interesting that her name should be so constantly linked with James's, considering how different were their approaches to their art. His influence is visible, superficially, in her early work, and, of course, they were both interested in Americans in Europe, but there the resemblance ceases. James was subtle, speculative, and indirect; Edith Wharton was always clear and to the point. Percy Lubbock speaks of her aversion to the abstract, to any discussion of the conundrum of life's meaning. She dealt with definite psychological and social problems and handled them in her own definite way. Her sentences never have to be read and reread, like James's, for richer and deeper disclosures. Furthermore, she and James, although good friends, never appreciated the best in each other's work. He found her most successful when most under his influence, as, for example, in *The Reef*, while she distrusted the whole artistic bent of his later years, feeling that he was severing himself more and more from "that thick nourishing human air in which we all live and move." If she must be regarded as anyone's disciple, it would be more accurate to note her relation to George Eliot, whose clear, strong style, broad canvas, and obsession with moral questions always fascinated her.

As long as Mrs. Wharton had elected, after the war, to continue writing about the social life of a city that she had given up even visiting, she would have done better to restrict herself to the eras of its history with which she was acquainted. The four stories that make up *Old New York* (1924) evoke the atmosphere of the last century as successfully as anything in *The Age of Innocence*. But she was too concerned with the world around her to write only of the past. She wanted nothing less than to interpret the age in which she lived and to seek out the origin and cause of the increasing number of things in it that angered her. Also, her way of life had become expensive — a house north of Paris, another on the Riviera, twenty-two servants — and she needed a wider audience. To take advantage of the big pay of the American women's magazines, it was necessary to write about Americans of the moment.

The Glimpses of the Moon (1922) was first serialized in the *Pictorial Review*, which may give the clue to its author's remarkable lapse of style and taste. The jacket of the book depicts an Italian villa on Lake Como by moonlight to evoke the mawkish, gushing mood of an opening chapter which makes the reader rub his eyes and look again to be sure that he is dealing with Edith Wharton. Nick and Susy Lansing, two bright young penniless hangers-on of the international set, have married on the understanding that their bond may be dissolved at the option of the first to find a richer spouse. Nick is again the dilettante hero, writing a novel about Alexander the Great in Asia because it takes less research than an essay, but now, for the first time, reader and author see him from radically different points of view. To the reader he is, quite simply, an unmitigated cad, perfectly content to live in the borrowed houses of rich friends so long as his wife agrees not to steal the cigars or to take any overt part in the blindfolding of their hostesses' deceived husbands. On these two commandments hang all his law and his prophets, and when Susy has violated both (in each case, for his sake), he abruptly abandons her to pursue an heiress. It is impossible to imagine how Mrs. Wharton could have picked such a man as the hero of a romance unless she seriously believed that he represented what a gentleman had sunk to in the seventeen years which had elapsed since the publication of *The House of Mirth*. But could even Lawrence Selden have degenerated to a Nick Lansing? And could Lily Bart ever have stolen cigars? Surely the world had not been entirely taken over by the Lansings and their dismal set of international drifters who blur together in a maze of furs and jewels and yachts. Mrs. Wharton's preoccupation with vulgarity had for the moment vulgarized her perceptions.

The lapse in her style can be illustrated by contrasting three descriptions of ladies of fashion. The first is from *The House of Mirth*. Lawrence Selden is taking his shrewd, leisurely note of the person of Lily Bart, and his speculations provide our first insight into the central problem of her character: "Everything about her was at once vigorous and exquisite, at once strong and fine. He had a confused sense that she must have cost a great deal to make, that a great many dull and ugly people must, in some mysterious way, have been sacrificed to produce her. He was aware that the qualities distinguishing her from the herd of her sex were chiefly external: as though a fine glaze of beauty and fastidiousness had been applied to vulgar clay."

The second is from the scene in *Madame de Treymes*, published two years later, where John Durham contemplates Fanny de Malrive after her call upon his mother and sister at their hotel and discerns in her fluster a ground for hope as to his future. The passage, with a faint Jamesian ring, is finely conceived: "The mere fact of her having forgotten to draw on her gloves as they were descending in the hotel lift from his mother's drawing-room was, in this connection, charged with significance to Durham. She was the kind of woman who always presents herself to the mind's eye as completely equipped, as made of exquisitely cared for and finely-related details; and that the heat of her parting with his family should have left her unconscious that she was emerging gloveless into Paris, seemed, on the whole, to speak hopefully for Durham's future opinion of the city."

Turning to *The Glimpses of the Moon*, we see one of Susy Lansing's friends, not only through Susy's eyes, but through the angrily disapproving eyes of Mrs. Wharton. The idea to be conveyed is that the lady described is as banal as her motor and her motor as banal as a magazine advertisement, but as the style is literally the style of a magazine advertisement, we can only wonder what reason the author has to sneer: "But on the threshold a still more familiar figure met her: that of a lady in exaggerated pearls and sables, descending from an exaggerated motor, like the motors in magazine advertisements, the huge arks in which jeweled beauties and slender youths pause to gaze at snow-peaks from an Alpine summit."

Fortunately the novels that followed *The Glimpses of the Moon* are not all quite as slick. If they are not good novels, neither are they potboilers. But it seems a pity that Mrs. Wharton should have chosen to lay all the blame for the shapelessness of the postwar world on her native land. In book after book her complaints grow shriller and shriller until at last everything across the Atlantic is tainted with the same grotesque absurdity. She gives to her American towns such names as Delos, Aeschylus, Lohengrin, and Halleluja, and to their inhabitants, in their brief hours away from money-making, a total gullibility in dealing with religious and medical charlatans. Their fuzzy zeal for good causes envelops their hideous skyscrapers in a stifling cloud of euphoria. And the American face! How it haunts her! It is as "unexpressive as a football." It might have been made by "a manufacturer of sporting goods." Its sameness encompasses her "with its innocent uniformity." How many of such faces would it take "to make up a single individuality"? Years before, she had written to an English friend about James: "America can't be quite so summarily treated and so lightly dismissed as our great Henry thinks." Yet, reading her later novels, we can only wish that she had dismissed America altogether.

Kate Clephane in *The Mother's Recompense* (1925) returns to a society in New York which has ostracized her, as it ostracized Mrs. Lidcote in "Autre Temps," to find, unlike Mrs. Lidcote, that it *can* revise its judgments. She is completely accepted by the people who once cut her and thinks the less of them for their tolerance. She finds only one person in New York who seems to have any real moral fiber, and that is her daughter who, perhaps for the same reason, strikes the reader as a rather wooden girl. When Kate discovers that Anne is ignorantly about to marry her own former lover, she tries desperately to break up the match without telling the girl why and finally surrenders to the situation in order to avoid "sterile pain." But having renounced sterile pain for her daughter, she elects it for herself by refusing the offer of marriage from a devoted old admirer who has been shocked, but only momentarily, by her confession.

Mrs. Wharton resented the critics who deplored the ending of the book and spoke of the "densities of incomprehension" with which she now felt herself surrounded. The clue to Kate's sacrifice, she hinted, lies in the quotation from Shelley on the flyleaf: "Desolation is a delicate thing." My own interpretation is that

Kate, imbued with the sensitivity of one who, like Mrs. Lidcote, has been broken on the wheel of a sterner age, feels more keenly than anyone else the horror of Anne's marriage. What she hates in the modern world is not so much that such things can happen as that people no longer really care that they do. Anne is caught in the situation of marrying her mother's lover because her mother has *had* a lover, and for that there must be expiation on the mother's part, alone in her shabby Riviera village, without the comfort of her old admirer. For Kate to go from the litter of fallen rose petals and grains of rice of her daughter's wedding to her own would be joining forces with the noisy, thoughtless world of vacuous toasts in which all delicacy of feeling has vanished. Those who believe in the old, harder standards must be willing to suffer alone, without sympathy or even comprehension. But this, evidently, is not sterile pain. Kate Clephane is intended to inhale a finer aroma from the bouquet of her loneliness than her daughter will ever know.

So far Mrs. Wharton had only skirmished with America. The story of the Lansings takes place in Europe, and Kate Clephane's drama is too much of the heart to have the locality of first importance. But she was preparing herself for a closer study of what had happened to America, and she had now spotted a type that she considered a representative victim of the disease of modern vulgarity, if, indeed, it was not the virus itself. Pauline Manford in *Twilight Sleep* (1927) is the daughter of an invader from "Exploit" who has first been married to a son of the age of innocence, Arthur Wyant. But time has profoundly altered both types. The invader's daughter is no longer prehensile or even crude; she has become bland and colorless and pointlessly efficient, building a life of public speeches and dinner parties around causes that she does not even try to understand, while Wyant, no longer the cool, well-dressed New York gentleman with a collector's eye for painting and porcelain, has degenerated to a foolish gossiping creature whom his wife has understandably divorced for a sneaky affair with his mother's old-maid companion. That is what has come of the merger of the old and new societies; it has cost each its true character. Pauline Manford, with invader's blood, has survived better than has Wyant, but hers is a lonely and precarious survival in a rosy cloud floating on an ether of fatuity from which she views with frightened eyes the moral collapse of her family. The invaders and their daughters have in common the faculty of immense preoccupation, the former with their businesses, the latter with their causes. But both are blinded to all that is beautiful or significant in the world around them by the dust stirred up by their febrile activities.

In Mrs. Manford Edith Wharton was groping at the outline of a well-known American phenomenon, the committeewoman who, married to a man who cares only for his business, seeks refuge in bogus Utopias where beauty is expected to spring like a phoenix from the ashes of pain. If Mrs. Wharton had only stayed in America, how quickly she would have comprehended such a woman! But Mrs. Manford is nothing but a caricature, mixing up her speeches to the birth control league and the society for unlimited families, going to the "Busy Man's Christ" for "uplift" treatments and seeing her children only by secretarial appointment. Mrs. Wharton seems to have no sense of the violent resentment that may underlie such a woman's placid stare or of the hatred of spouse and possessive passion for offspring that her false air of good sportsmanship may conceal. The American committeewoman is not apt, like Mrs. Manford, to be surrounded by a family who regard her goings-on merely with a cheerful, amused tolerance. *Twilight Sleep* is a formidable battering ram used on a straw woman.

There was to be one more last grim sketch of the final decadence resulting from the now ancient merger between old New York and the invaders. In the short story "After Holbein," a senile Mrs. Jaspar sits down alone every night at the end of her great dining room table, imagining that she is still the hostess at a dinner party, while her smirking servants go through a pantomime of serving guests. Anson Warley, a veteran bachelor, dilettante, and diner out, who has scorned her parties in the days of her greatness, suffering now himself from loss of memory, goes to her house by mistake, and the two old broken-down creatures squeak and gibber together, drinking the soda water which they take for Perrier-Jouet and admiring flower vases stuffed with old newspapers. It has been said that there is no compassion in this story, but how much compassion does a short story need? It is a chilling, cleverly executed little piece, a sort of dance of death, pointing a grim moral in the ultimate inanity of two lives dedicated to the ceremonial of the dinner party.

American mothers she had now done, together with their husbands, both of the invader and dilettante variety, but what about children? They had never played much of a role in her books, as, indeed, they had played little in her life. Mrs. Winthrop Chanler has written that she was actually afraid of them. But if she was ignorant of American nurseries and schools, she was very much aware of those pathetic little waifs, the products of multiple marriages, who were dragged about Europe in the wake of rich, pleasure-seeking parents and finally abandoned with governesses in seaside hotels. The various Wheater offspring in *The Children* (1928) have sworn to remain together under the lead of Judith, the eldest, in spite of what other custody arrangements their various parents and "steps" may make. The children are sometimes amusingly, sometimes touchingly drawn, but the sketches are still superficial and "cute," and the background of rich expatriate life in European resorts is filled in with the now heavy hand of her satire.

The more interesting though secondary topic of the book is

the relationship between Rose Sellars, the quiet, gentle widow of exquisite tact, with whom I suspect Mrs. Wharton may have a bit identified herself, and Martin Boyne, again the tasteful middle-aged bachelor, who has made a fortune, like other Wharton heroes, offstage and has now plenty of time to idle abroad. Rose Sellars immediately understands and accepts the fact that Boyne's pre-occupation with the Wheater children is, unknown to himself, a manifestation of his hopeless passion for little Judith. The novel was published in the year that followed Walter Berry's death, and the relationship between the two characters seems analogous to what may have existed between their creator and Berry: she, loving and eager, but restrained by the fear of embarrassing them both by a scene that might expose the small beer of his feeling, and he, detached but admiring, half disappointed and half irritated at his own inability to respond to a gratifying if sometimes cloying affection. It is tempting to speculate that Martin Boyne's fate is the author's revenge on his deceased counterpart. We leave him in the end, old and desolate, staring through a ballroom window at the beautiful Judith who, dancing with young men, is no longer even aware of his existence.

After *The Children* Edith Wharton embarked, although then in her late sixties, on the most ambitious experiment of her literary career: the fictional biography of a young middle western American writer, Vance Weston, told in two novels: *Hudson River Bracketed* (1929) and *The Gods Arrive* (1932). She opens his story in a town which is, typically enough, called "Euphoria" and plunges fearlessly into details of middle western life, as if Sinclair Lewis by dedicating *Babbitt* to her had given her some special insight into an area of America that she had never even seen. The result is as bad as might be expected, but Vance Weston soon leaves his home town and comes to New York and an old house on the Hudson where his creator is on more familiar ground and where he meets a highly accomplished young lady, Halo Spear, who recites German poetry to him. "Just listen to the sound of the words," she says, when he protests his ignorance of the tongue.

It is easy to ridicule this long saga with its distorted picture of the New York publishing world, its uncouth young writers and artists ("Zola — who's he?" somebody yawned. "Oh, I dunno. The French Thackeray, I guess."), its irritatingly efficient heroine who can change travel accommodations and rent villas as easily as she can spout Goethe, its insensitive hero whose obsessive egotism becomes ultimately tedious, its ponderous satires of popular novelists and literary hostesses, but it nonetheless contains a strong picture of a young genius who educates himself and fights his way to literary success with a ruthlessness of which he is too preoccupied to be more than dimly aware. We sympathize when he is stifled in the ignorant, carping atmosphere of his invalid first wife's home and with his artist's need to rip away even at the most basic family ties. Here at last in Edith Wharton's fiction is a picture of a man. It may have all kinds of personal significance that he is neither a New Yorker nor a gentleman. As he develops cultivation in Europe, however, he develops some of the hardness of the older Wharton heroes, and when he leaves Halo at last for a round of parties in London, there is not much to choose between him and Martin Boyne. But that is in the second volume which, like so many sequels, should never have been written. Both reader and author have become bored with Vance. Yet one cannot but be impressed by the fund of creative energy that could produce such a book on such a subject in the author's seventieth year.

At the very end of her life Edith Wharton turned back once again to the rich field of her childhood memories, and immediately the shrill bitterness disappears, and the old, clear, forceful style is back to the aid of its mistress. If she had finished *The Buccaneers* (1938) it might well rank among the best of her work. The little band of social-climbing maidens who find New York too difficult and leave it to triumph in London are unique in her fiction as possessing both her approval and affection. Old New York seems merely petty and narrow now in the person of Mrs. Parmore, while the parvenu is actually given charm and vitality in that of Colonel St. George. The author's point of view is expressed by the English governess of the St. George girls, Laura Testvalley, an erudite but romantic spinster of Italian descent, a cousin of the Rossettis, who adores her covey of Daisy Millers and guides them up the slippery rungs of the London social ladder. Until the girls have achieved their titles the mood of the book is light and amusing; thereafter it becomes more serious. For they have, after all, missed happiness, and Nan, as the author's notebooks reveal, will find hers only by leaving the Duke of Tintagel for Guy Thwarte.

Mrs. Wharton had not only cast aside for once her disapproval of those who are discontented to remain in the social grade of their origin; she had even cast off four decades of classicism in taste and morals to plot an ending that was to celebrate the triumph of "deep and abiding love." Yet how many times in her stories and novels have we not been told that no love can survive the cold shoulder of society, the disintegrating shabbiness of a life in second-class watering places! And is Nan now to get away with it, to escape the fate of Anna Karenina?

But if Mrs. Wharton, at the end, permitted herself to indulge in the vision of a love that was to make up for everything, the love that Ellen Olenska and Newland Archer had renounced, she was still enough of a Yankee puritan to stipulate that such a love had to be paid for. If Nan and Guy are to have their happiness, Laura Testvalley must lose hers. Her engagement to Guy's father will not survive her role in his son's elopement. Laura, the author's representative and a bit her alter ego, must be sacrificed to the gods of order. One wonders if at the last those gods did not, to Laura's

41

creator, show some of the lineaments of the gods of derision whom she had so bitterly apostrophized in her journal thirty years before.

With her posthumously published works, *The Buccaneers* and *Ghosts,* the total of Edith Wharton's fiction comes to thirty-two volumes. Obviously, her ultimate reputation in American letters will rest upon only a fraction of this list. *Ethan Frome,* I have no doubt, will always be read, but it is out of the main stream of her work. I believe that she will be remembered primarily for her two great novels of manners: *The House of Mirth,* and *The Age of Innocence.* In these she succeeded in re-creating an unadventurous and ceremonious society, appropriately sheltered behind New York brownstone, looking always to the east rather than to the west, and the impact upon it of the winds that blew from both directions. There were plenty of minor writers who attempted to delineate this society, but among those of the first rank Mrs. Wharton, at least in the first decade of our century, had it to herself. It is true, of course, that some of James's characters come from the same milieu, but they are rarely considered in relation to their native land or cities. The reason Mrs. Wharton succeeded where so many others have failed is that in addition to her gifts as an artist she had a firm grasp of what "society," in the smaller sense of the word, was actually made up of. She understood that it was arbitrary, capricious, and inconsistent; she was aware that it did not hesitate to abolish its standards while most loudly proclaiming them. She knew when money could open doors and when it couldn't, when lineage would serve and when it would be merely sneered at. She knew that compromises could be counted on, but that they were rarely made while still considered compromises. She knew her men and women of property, recently or anciently acquired, how they decorated their houses and where they spent their summers. She realized that the social game was without rules, and this realization made her one of the few novelists before

Proust who could describe it with any profundity. In American
fiction her nearest counterpart is Ellen Glasgow.

Edith Wharton died in her house near Paris of a stroke in 1937,
at the age of seventy-five. Her private papers were given to Yale
and may not be published before 1968, which is probably the reason no biography has yet appeared. A great deal has been written
about her in articles and memoirs, but almost always about the
great lady, rarely the writer. This is nobody's fault, for Mrs. Wharton took a certain pride in keeping her writing behind the scenes,
in presenting herself to the world, so to speak, on her own. One
short piece, however, by Iris Origo, describes a weekend on Long
Island that Mrs. Wharton spent with old friends during a brief
visit to America to receive a degree from Yale. It is one of the rare
recorded occasions when the survivor from New York's age of
innocence, the real figure behind the novelist, predominated over
the brilliant and formidable lady of perfect houses and gardens.
Iris Origo relates how Mrs. Wharton refused to be led into any discussion of persons or events in France, of Carlo Placi or Madame
de Noailles, and how, at each such attempt, she gently and firmly
steered the conversation back to old friends and old memories in
New York. The W's house on 11th Street, had it really been pulled
down? Did her hostess remember the night they had dined there
before the Colony Club ball? The X's daughter, the fair one, had
she married her young Bostonian? Had Z indeed lost all his money?

"For the whole evening, this mood continued. At one moment
only — as, the last guest gone, she turned half-way up the stairs to
wave good-night — I caught a glimpse of the other Edith: elegant,
formidable, as hard and dry as porcelain. Then, as she looked
down on her old friends, her face softened, even the erectness of her
spine relaxed a little. She was no longer the trim, hard European
hostess, but a nice old American lady. Edith had come home."

✓ Selected Bibliography

Works of Edith Wharton

NOVELS AND COLLECTIONS OF SHORT STORIES

The Greater Inclination. New York: Scribner's, 1899.

The Touchstone. New York: Scribner's, 1900.

Crucial Instances. New York: Scribner's, 1901.

The Valley of Decision. New York: Scribner's, 1902.

Sanctuary. New York: Scribner's, 1903.

The Descent of Man and Other Stories. New York: Scribner's, 1904.

The House of Mirth. New York: Scribner's, 1905.

Madame de Treymes. New York: Scribner's, 1907.

The Fruit of the Tree. New York: Scribner's, 1907.

The Hermit and the Wild Woman and Other Stories. New York: Scribner's, 1908.

Tales of Men and Ghosts. New York: Scribner's, 1910.

Ethan Frome. New York: Scribner's, 1911.

The Reef. New York: Appleton, 1912.

The Custom of the Country. New York: Scribner's, 1913.

Xingu and Other Stories. New York: Scribner's, 1916.

Summer. New York: Appleton, 1917.

The Marne. New York: Appleton, 1918.

The Age of Innocence. New York: Appleton, 1920.

The Glimpses of the Moon. New York: Appleton, 1922.

A Son at the Front. New York: Scribner's, 1923.

Old New York: False Dawn (The 'Forties); The Old Maid (The 'Fifties); The Spark (The 'Sixties); New Year's Day (The 'Seventies). New York: Appleton, 1924.

The Mother's Recompense. New York: Appleton, 1925.

Here and Beyond. New York: Appleton, 1926.

Twilight Sleep. New York: Appleton, 1927.

The Children. New York: Appleton, 1928.

Hudson River Bracketed. New York: Appleton, 1929.

Certain People. New York: Appleton, 1930.

The Gods Arrive. New York: Appleton, 1932.

Human Nature. New York: Appleton, 1933.

The World Over. New York: Appleton-Century, 1936.

Ghosts. New York: Appleton-Century, 1937.

The Buccaneers. New York: Appleton-Century, 1938.

POETRY

Verses. Newport, R.I.: C. E. Hammett, Jr., 1878.
Artemis to Actaeon and Other Verse. New York: Scribner's, 1909.
Twelve Poems. London: The Medici Society, 1926.

NONFICTION

The Decoration of Houses (with Ogden Codman, Jr.). New York: Scribner's, 1897.
Italian Villas and Their Gardens. New York: Century, 1904.
Italian Backgrounds. New York: Scribner's, 1905.
A Motor-Flight through France. New York: Scribner's, 1908.
Fighting France, from Dunkerque to Belfort. New York: Scribner's, 1915.
French Ways and Their Meaning. New York: Appleton, 1919.
In Morocco. New York: Scribner's, 1920.
The Writing of Fiction. New York: Scribner's, 1925.
A Backward Glance. New York: Appleton-Century, 1934.

TRANSLATIONS

The Joy of Living. By Hermann Sudermann. New York: Scribner's, 1902.

COMPILATIONS

The Book of the Homeless. New York: Scribner's, 1916.
Eternal Passion in English Poetry (with Robert Norton and Gaillard Lapsley). New York: Appleton-Century, 1939.

CURRENT AMERICAN REPRINTS

Ethan Frome. New York: Scribner's. $1.25.
The Age of Innocence. New York: Modern Library. $1.95.
The House of Mirth. New York: Scribner's. $1.45.

Critical and Biographical Studies

Andrews, Wayne. Introduction to *The Best Short Stories of Edith Wharton.* New York: Scribner's, 1958.
Brooks, Van Wyck. *The Confident Years.* New York: Dutton, 1952.
Browne, E. K. *Edith Wharton, Etude Critique.* Paris: Librairie E. Droz, 1935.
Edel, Leon. "Edith Wharton," in *The Dictionary of American Biography,* Volume 22. New York: Scribner's, 1958.
James, Henry. *Letters to Walter Berry.* Paris: Black Sun Press, 1928.
Kazin, Alfred. *On Native Grounds.* New York: Reynal and Hitchcock, 1942.

Lubbock, Percy. *Portrait of Edith Wharton.* New York: Appleton-Century-Crofts, 1947.

Nevius, Blake. *Edith Wharton, A Study of Her Fiction.* Berkeley and Los Angeles: University of California Press, 1953.

Origo, Iris. "The Homecoming." *New Statesman and Nation,* February 16, 1957.

Wilson, Edmund. *The Wound and the Bow.* Boston: Houghton Mifflin, 1941

———. *Classics and Commercials.* New York: Farrar, Straus, 1950.